Millie's Poems

Millie's Poems

Butch Raul

authorHOUSE®

AuthorHouse™
1663 Liberty Drive
Bloomington, IN 47403
www.authorhouse.com
Phone: 1 (800) 839-8640

Published by AuthorHouse   11/03/2015

ISBN: 978-1-5049-1597-7 (sc)
ISBN: 978-1-5049-1596-0 (e)

Contents

MONEY

Money, money, money
Who's got the money?
Money on the whole
Money comes and goes.
Most of the time it
doesn't even stay,
to make your day!
Money, Money, Money.
There it goes again.
Not taking time to
be my friend.
Author
Butch Raul
1-23-2015

MOVING ON IN LIFE

As the casket is closed,
we tend to coast.
Wondering what was the most
of the love that everyone boast.

Jesus tried
Oh how He cried
when His child went to hide
from the world's changing tide.
Author
Butch Raul

MOVING

One days blues is
Mondays moves
packing and hacking
wacking and stacking
moving and groving is
what it's all about.
Author
Butch Raul
6-13-2006

MY GOD

My God how sweet tho art.
With love in Your heart,
You want Your people to
turn to You and not fall
apart.
With love for others,You
help Mothers and brothers.
Sister's come with Your
love dancing in the clouds
above.
Author
Butch Raul
2-22-2014

An Ode To Nikki

My Little Sweet Pea

My little sweet pea
Won't cha wait for me?
Flying around as happy as can be.
Pretty little sweet pea fly back to me.
I'll hold you in my heart forever.
With your free soul to go where ever.
I'll set you free when you grow up,
but don't fall on the buttercup.
Whoa, sweet pea fly around the tree.
You're so beautiful everyone can see,
Your God's creation and you'll always be
My, "Little Sweet Pea."
Love Mom & Mom2
Author
Butch Raul
3-6-2015

My Shopping Buddy

My shopping buddy and I had a lot of fun.
We would always be on the run.
We would go from store to store.
Sometimes we would buy little and sometimes
more.
As years flew by we would always try to get
together, no matter what the weather.
Than we moved apart and that broke our hearts.
Now we get on the phone and tell each other
where we roam.
Author
Butch Raul
12-4-204

My Sister

My sister is gone
there's no holding on.
She suffers no more.
God closed the door.
He took her home.
Now she can really
roam.
Author
Butch Raul
2-22-2014
Joyce R's
sunset happemed at
10:00 a.m.

Never to Last

Never to last, passing so fast.
Are the memories of yester year.
Happy are the days of old.
When the sad ones are not told.
People pull at your past like
a bag of trash.
A word will pass like broken glass.
There you will be on your broken knee.
Broken spirit and very low on self control.
You look in to the mirror and see your
face, and know this is not your place.
Author
Butch Raul
9-15-1994

No Fight Left

I want to cry, I know not why-
there is a pit of emptiness,
resting hard on my chest.

I have no fight left to face my day.
I don't how to walk away.
My mind goes blank in dismay,
what could I do this hollow way?

Go to church my mind does say,
on this cold October day;
for there may not be many times
till May.
Author
Butch Raul
10-21-1995

No Love to Find

No flowers to grow,
No words to show.
No love to find,
to say what's on my mind.
His heart above,
carries you like a dove.
With staff in hand,
He holds you like a lamb.
By the still waters you lie,
so weak you think you should die.
Only He pats your head and says,
"There my little one just stay
as life goes by, I will show you the way."
Author
Butch Raul
11-09-2000

No One In Sight

No one in sight,

But letters to write.

My friends all around,

I'm just house bound.

I like my place,

Who can set the pace.

I walk the halls,

So I won't be big this fall.

God put Your hand on my heart,

so it doesn't fall apart.

I have to be strong,

my friend needs me now,

so I can help her somehow.

Author

Butch Raul

2-28-2014

OCTOBER TO MAY

I want to cry, I know not why.
There is a pit of emptiness
resting deep in my chest.
I have to fight to face my day,
I don't know how to walk away.
Go to church my mind does say,
on this October day.
Circumstance has it not,
to wonder why I'm so distraught.
My toe in the air,no one will dare
to step on it and give it flare.
So to church I say nay and ask
God to find His way to make
a house call today and all the
way to May.
Author
Butch Raul
2008

ONE NEVER KNOWS

One never knows,
who a special friend is.

One never knows,
What that special friend is going to do.

One never knows,
what a special friend is there for.

One never knows,
what that friend is feeling.

One never knows,
how long that special friend is going
to last.
Author
Butch Raul
7-12-2013

OUT OF THE BLUE

Out of the blue
Out of school
wanting to write
what a fright
unable to spell
I can still wish
them well.
Author
Butch Raul
5-16-2007

PHYSICAL THERAPY

Physical therapy is not the place to be,
unless you have the heart to see,how good
the workers are to you and me.

They push us to pains degree and we know
it hurts to be the one behind the broken
knee.

Our worker's are there for all physical
therapy we need, and we are happy they
stand their ground, when we find we are
walking around.

We give thanks to our physical therapy
workers as we go on our own to be,
telling everyone how good the physical
therapy was for you and me.

Author

Butch Raul

11-1-2002

POOR LITTLE RABBIT

Poor little rabbit tore apart
so lonesome healing from a broke heart.
so far away and all alone, Its mama
wants him to come home.
Mended from all the broken parts, soon
to be back in his mama's arms.
Never to leave his cart.
P.S. Poor Little Rabbit went through
the washing machine & got ripped & frail.
You see Poor Little Rabbit is a doll.
Author
Butch Raul
8-23-2014

RAG DOLL

This doll is frayed and pulled apart.
She has arms that no one wants around them.
Her feet turn the wrong way.
Causing her legs to twist and bend, then
on her bottom she does end.
She had a heart full of love,
that no one wanted any of.
Empty as can be, she hopes somehow
to see someone to need her love endlessly.

Author

Butch Raul

READING

Reading my books
leads me to the brooks.
Watching water flow,
eases my soul.
Hearing God's voice
gives me a choice
of listening to His
words and then the
pen touches the page.

Author
Butch Raul
5-13-2014

REJECTION

Rejection, what a life reflection,
Alone at first who could be the worst.
Unwanted by the mother and the others.
Put on display while kids run and play.
Fight for life that is my strife.

Author

Butch Raul

7-7-1992

Ring Ring

Ring, ring, Hello
Who's on the other end?
none other then my long
distance friend.
Hello
I know how wonderful it
is to stay in touch, I
love you so much.
Author
Butch Raul
6-18-2006

Running and Hiding

Spying and trying.
Running and hiding.
No!
Moving and grooving.
Not!
Shaking and baking.
Is more liking the aching!
Mending and bending.
Sealing and realing.
Yea
Winding and binding,
is the hope of it all.
Author
Butch Raul
5-11-1999

RUNNING AND WRITING

Running and writing
is what I do best.
It helps me get things
off my chest.

Praying and saying
things to the Lord,
Sure keeps me from
being bored.

Talking and walking
with my Father above,
is what gave me shove.
Author
Butch Raul
9-11-2014

SEWING CLOTHES

Sewing clothes
making bows
toy rabbits
just a habit
seeing joy in
every girl and boy.
Author
Butch Raul
7-20-2006

Singing In The Breeze

Walking past the trees.
Singing in the breeze.
Lighting the load
I piled it in the road.
Reaching out my hand,
Letting Jesus have the stand.
Author
Butch Raul
7-24-1998

SISTER OR MOTHER

Sister or mother
which will it be?
You can love me,
which ever you see.
I had a mother and
I love her like no
other.
I had a brother,
how he hovered.
and I do miss him so.
Not a mother or brother,
but my sister;who do
you think has my heart
through all this ink.
Author
Butch Raul
9-21-1998

Slam Door Friend

She's there at the end, my slam door friend.

wash day blues,who could snooze.

Dog in the corner, none to warn her.

Shut our face T.J. dog had to jump.

Basket bound, what a hound.

How well he minds, I want to show you mine.

Poodle pup, what a chump.

Bring him to the house, I want to show my spouse.

I set the pace, what a waste.

From the door to the floor.

Five minutes stand. I'll give a hand.

Ice cold heart, she tore it apart.

It may not rhyme,but it sure shows the time.

How God gave His grace to show His pace.

From hell bent to heaven bound. God used you
to turn me around. You did not frown.

You stood your ground.

Author

Butch Raul

2-2-1999

SLEEPLESS

Sleepless night

Empty sights
In the dark
Hearing dog's bark
Where's the sleep
Without a peep
gone away
up drinking coffee
I want it morning
don't ya see?
Author
Butch Raul
4-27-2006

SPRING OR SUMMER

Spring or summer
Winter or fall,
tell me which one do
you like best of all.
Inside or out,the
world begin to
sprout.
Come over here,
look what is growing
so dear.
Or look at the hay,
it has turned so gray.
Then another year begins.
Author
Butch Raul
3-9-2002

Sue D Q

Sue D Q
You're my sister
You're my friend
You're my one an
only kin.
We lost our mother,
We lost our brother.
I hope not to lose
No other.
Christ will come
one day,
I hope it's not
in May.
Only God has that
say
Author
Butch Raul
2-27-2014

THANK YOU GOD

Thank you God for helping
me pull through.
Thank you God for holding
my hand.
Thank you God for taking
a stand.
Thank you God for my
family
Author
Butch Raul
2-27-2014

THE LAST RIDE

Though it may be on wheels go I,
my chariot awaits me.
I'm going to my home above,
to be in my Father's love.
Weep not for me cause,
there will be someone you'll see.
His love for me will never fail,
I have to walk that long trail.
Author
Butch Raul
6-18-2002

THE TRAILER AT THE END OF THE ROAD

The trailer at the end of the road, how
lonely, how old.
Is it kept up or run down?
The road is paved and rocky
There's no telling how it will go.
Does it hold young or old? The trees
holding it together are saplings.
Not a wind break standing there
at the end of the road.
Author
Butch Raul
5-26-2013

The Trip

Baking and aching
When words are breaking
My heart is breaking apart.
Over the road home is where
I want to be, the trip was
not fun to me.
Hurtful words were said.
I just wanted to hang my head.
Author
Butch Raul
12-28-2014

THE WORD

With books all around,
My Bible bound.

Through the word I search,
My mind can not be in the lurch.

Oh Lord my eyes,
Please give them the surprise.

Food for my soul,
can only make me whole.

I have such a problem,
I can't reach out to save them.

You put the words there.
so I don't despair.

How wonderful you are,
to travel so far.
Author
Butch Raul
7-13-2007

There's No Words

There's no words to make us work.
There's no word's to heal the soul.
Bitterness abounds
Emptiness surrounds
as we try
time goes by
then
we try again.
Then we open the door
and God takes the floor.
Author
Butch Raul
2-24-2000

TO MY FRIEND

To my friend
this is the end
So far as I know
nothing left to show.
But as poems go on this
to I just made this up
must go on, on the spot.
Love to all.
Author
Butch Raul
2-4-2014

TO THE MOTHER YOU WANTED TO BE

To the mother you wanted to be
I was blind and could not see
all the signs you gave to me.
You showed your heart as best
you could, but someone else
stoled your place.
Now it's years down the road
and a sister's love is what
I need, so to you I give the
deed.
Author
Butch Raul
4-28-2014

Tuff Stuff

Loners are made of tuff stuff,
so others realy believe.
As a loner, per say, I have been told
by so many people that I was made of
tuff stuff-and that I was a survivor!

Rocks and mountains are made out of
tuff stuff also, but the winds are to
mountains and rocks as words are to people.
The slightest of each could cause the
fall of all the tuff stuff.
Author
Mildred L. Raul
9-16-1996

TWO HANDS

Two hands
to hold
Two hands
to fold
Two hands
to show us
how to pray.
Butch Raul
6-17-1997

Friend Material

How to know friend material.
When that person is a friend of a friend.
One listens to them and sees what one's
friend sees.

How to know friend material.
when that person is open and honest.
One sees the truth in one's new friend.
My friend, that is you.
Author
Butch Raul
9-1-2013

WATCHING THE TIME

Watching the time slip by.
I doodly pray,
"God help me on this day."
Looking at the little glob so small.
Wondering how God can see us all.

He sees His glory turn to trash,
No wonder He wants to turn it to ash.
Dirt and filth the people have slung,
this world has no place for the young.
Author
Butch Raul
5-20-1998

WHAT A TRUE FRIEND "WON'T" SAY OR DO

Here's my number, but don't call me I'll call you.

Here is how to reach me, Don't call me.

I have things to do.

I'll be at #_____,but don't call me. I'm working

all the time.

Have you heard from_____?

Don't call me, I'll be away from my phone.

I thought I would see your number on my scanner,

I'm glad I didn't, I was out of range.

From people who wanted me to stay in touch...HA!

Author

Butch Raul

2007

What is A Friend

What is a friend?
A friend is someone who is there
when your healthy or sick.

What is a friend?
Someone who is there no
matter what you have done.

What is a friend?
A friend is someone who will
cry with you when your sad and
laugh with you when your happy.

What is a friend?
Someone who will
hold your hair
when you are sick.

That my friend is you.
Author
Butch Raul
8-30-2013

WONDERING

Wondering if yer here or there.
Ya can wonder into a truck, or ya can
wonder around like a duck.
Ya can wonder if yer here, or ya can
wonder if yer there. How ever ya
wonder,ya best find out what yer won-
dering about
Author
Butch Raul
5-2-2006

WORDS THAT COME

Words that come and words that go,
we can make them real slow.
We can sing them in a song or speak
them all day long.
We can use them while we're pitching
hay or when we're taking time to pray.
We just hope most of all, they don't
cause someone to fall.

Author

Butch Raul

2-12-1999

You Never Know

You never know who's life you touch.
You never know what means so much.

You never see God's glory at work,
in that lonely heart that was hurt.

You do see the life that was turned around,
you do see they found their ground.

And pray to God that someday you'll see
the praise and thank Him for His glorious ways.
Author
Butch Raul

3-2-1988

You're Gone

You're gone, I'm so blue;
I don't know what to do.
Should I run or stay,or
just walk away.
In this empty nest,
I don't seem to get my rest.
Your gone from here,
I miss you so my dear.
How I love you so my friend.
Now I'll make this poem end.
Auther
Butch Raul
7-13-2013
From one friend to another.

YOUR LIFE

Angel's float about you hoping
you'll pull it together.
God is crying over you wanting
to help you through all your pain.
We know this is no game, fighting
for your life gives you no strife.
All our prayers touch God's heart
in hopes not to pull it apart.
Here on earth is not your home,
but we want you to be able to roam.
Come back to us soon, Get well so
you don't leave us in the gloom.
Your life is in the bloom.

Nikki we love you.Mom & Mom2

Author

Butch Raul

7-21-2013

My sweetheart Nikki Bowles (Nicol)
sunset was: 7-8-2013 of an infection
called Mercer.

A Friend to Me

A friend to me
Is hard to be
When in turmoil
I tend to coil.
Why must we gravel
When stormy seas we
travel?
Where is that friend
when we need a warming
trend?
Reaching out to hold my
hand, she knows not where
I stood.
Being so bold as she was
told.
To stand her ground,
I'll be found.
He will be the way
to guide the day.
God above gave the shove.
He took the stand,
He showed me your hand.
Author
Butch Raul
6-17-1997

A Life From The Past

A life from the past.
Who would have thought it could last.
The kind words that you said,
Little did we know where they lead.
Through the years ahead.
God knew the tears we would shed.
As life from the past,
is a treasure at last.
Author
Butch Raul
3-29-1999

A LONELY FOOL

It's a lonely world you were born in.
After you learn to walk and talk, you
get scorned.
There are people all around that adore you!
But the people that were around just bore you.
Now your old enough to go to school,you are
taught the golden rule.
You are taught to read and write, but that
doesn't help on a lonely night.
Author
Butch Raul
1977

To my Mom
Mildred L. Frost
My First Poem
Ever.

A Misfit

A misfit I may be,
My God watches over me.

Alone on this land,
He still carries me in His hand.

When the end is nigh,
I'll join Him in the sky.
Author
Butch Raul
11-3-1994

A Mother's Love

In her arms a mother holds her children.
She watches their every move and breath.
That's how love starts.

In her hands a mother guides her children.
She helps the dance and sing.
That's how love moves.

In her heart a mother cares for her children.
She hears their laughter and their cries.
That's how love grows.

As they are grown and on their own, the children
reach back to the hand and gives an arm to reach
the heart and show their mother their part.
That's how love goes.
Author
Butch Raul
1-7-1997

A New Leaf on My Tree of Life

A new leaf on my tree of life.
A new direction in my strife
leaving my security for adventure
to find out what God has in nature.

by
Butch Raul
4-21-2006

A POEM FOR YOU LORD

A poem for You Lord
a poem for you.
You are not the small babe
in a manger.
You're not even a stranger.
your birth gave a way
for people to share the day.
We should put You first,
because You came to earth
to show us we are sinners.
But through You we can be
winners.
Author
Butch Raul
12-19-2003

A SMALL CHILD

A small child
running wild.
A little whine
Killing time
with a little hope,
they won't smoke.
In the name of Jesus,
Please give your strength
to us.
how divine,
Now your mine.
Jesus smiles,
As He gives it to us.
Author
Butch Raul
10-24-1999

A Soft Touch

A soft touch is God's grace
As He moves through the breeze.
You can feel Him while your high
on a mountain or down in the valley.

A soft touch of the grass and the
ruffle of the leaves.
He's such a powerful wonderful spirit,
that can be so gentle and kind.
He is a powerful and mighty God,
when satan's on the prowl.

This God in heaven,My God
He is a wonderful loving God for me,
such a sinner to thee.
Author
Butch Raul
5-21-1998

A Time For Me Is Now

A time for me is now,
I'll go to the retreat somehow.
Lord help me watch the clouds
that float by so proud.

Help me heal so well,
I don't want to go to the well.
All of my friends will gather
at the lake, so I can't take a break.

Off to the farm I must go,
So soon to get me back into the flow.
Around and around I will fly,
in the airplane in the sky.

A time for me is now,
I will find my way somehow.
Thank you Lord; for the shove.
I need help from above.
Author
Butch Raul
6-13-2015

A True Friend

A true friend is there
through thick and thin and
in time a real friend
will sometime never end.
By
Butch Raul
8-3-2014

A Voice In The Night

Watching television and channel
Surfing, came a voice in
the night.
It touched my soul and said,
"Lets go to God in prayer."
A voice in the night
lead me back to the arms of
Jesus.
By
Butch Raul
2-12-1999

ALONE IN MY APARTMENT

Alone in my apartment
with my broken heart spent.

Then by my side,
Is my only guide.

My friend's give a hand,
As my relationship makes a stand.

God show me the way
to make it through the day.

He gives me His verse
So I don't turn worse.
Author
Butch Raul
2-27-1978

An Ode to Tysen

My Tysen

What a little dog
My Tysen was loving.
He wiggled his way
into my heart.
In his two years I had him,
he brought a lot of laughter
and tears to me.
He was 10 when he rescued me
from my broken world.
September 10,2012 was his
last day in my world.
He had a brain tumor
that caused his domain.
I loved my Mighty! Mighty!
TYSEN.
Author
Butch Raul
9-11-2012

Angel's Wings

Angel's wings,
cover us while

Angel's sing,
the sweetest things.
Angel's cry
when a person dies,
that is not one who tries.
Angle's sing with joy,
God has won another
soul when we give
up our earthly goals.
Author
Butch Raul
6-11-2005

AROUND WE GO

Around the world, around we go.

Down the road, down so slow,

A bumpy life, A bumpy blow,

and then again,

around the world, around we go.

by

Butch Raul

2-1-1990

BE STRONG

Help us be strong in Your ways
Dear Lord on this earthly day.
Build our hearts as we long
to sing of Your glory in a song.

by

Butch Raul

6-26-1998

BIG YOU LITTLE ME

The big you for little me, helped
me to call on Jesus.
The little me needs the big you to
help me to claim Jesus.
That way when the big you falls,the
little me can be strong and we both
can call to Jesus.
Jesus will show us that we are not
the black sheep of the family,we are
His prize possession.
He is our Shepard
Psalms 23
Author
Butch Raul
6-1-2000

Boo Boo Baby

Boo Boo Baby was my favorite doll.
Boo Boo Baby Had a bad fall.
Boo Boo Baby lost her nose.
Boo Boo Baby didn' know that I loved
her so. Oh I gave her away long ago.
Boo Boo Baby has a nice home.

Author

Butch Raul

6-21-2014

Bunny Time

This little bunny is here to say,
He's not the one that was on the tree.
He just wants to help you see,
what the day is to you and me.

The reason of easter is not for eggs
and candy.
'tis the day for Christ to be,
in our hearts for all to see.

As off to church we go, with
love for Him we know.
Jesus is not in the grave.
He has risen long ago,
in order to save our very soul.
Author
Butch Raul
4-17-1997

CAFE LIFE

Cafe life so easy, no just not very greasy.

Open the door, scrub the floor.

Mash potatoes, cutting tomatoes.

Who would know, how things would go,

Breakfast to lunch, what a crunch.

Mixing and cooking, baking and scraping,

Her pans pile up, Sharon B. fills her cup.

Time for a break, She never gets to take.

Lunch is done, now the supper run.

Author

Butch Raul

2-11-1999

CHRISTMAS GIFT

Christmas gifts use to be
as simple as love for you and me.
We would make things and stand
around and sing.
Now it is so commercial.
No one wants the usual.
No love for a brother,
No gift for one another.
What a craze life
Without Christ.
Author
Butch Raul
11-5-1999

CHEER UP IT'S CHRISTMAS TIME

Cheer up it's christmas time.
The season for all to enjoy family
and to let Christ back into your life.
So no one can give you strife.
Let your light for Christ shine and
don't think He is just mine.
Christ was born just in time to heal
our broken minds.
Author
Butch Raul
12-16-2014

COME LORD JESUS

Come Lord Jesus, be my guest.

As I lay me down to rest.

Let me sleep thru the night,

So the demon's don't give me fright.

Fill my mind with Your love.

So I know You're up above.

Author

Butch Raul

10-1-2014

CREAM PIE

Cream pie
want a slice?
have some rice,
That not nice.
by
Butch Raul
2-16-2000

DECISION

Good and bad.
We never know which we had.
Decisions don't let you think.
They just come on the blink.
Then it's to late.
You think was that my mate?
Am I this or that?
Oh goodness, where's my hat.
Author
Butch Raul
2-3-2015

DISASTER

`My kitchen is a disaster.
what am I here after?
Am I going to cook or
just take a look.
Where is my broom,
I need to clean this room.
Then next to know is
Where do these dishes go.
All cleaned up, now I can
fill up my cup.
Author
Butch Raul
10-2-2014

Do God's Work

Do God's work on earth,
and let Christ Jesus do
His work in you.
That won't get you to
heaven--- but it sure
won't hurt your chance.
Author
Butch Raul
2009

ED

I'm on the move again.

What a wonderful friend.

Ed didn't leave me on the limb.

He battled the wind.

With ice on the road,

He carried a heavy load.

Ed didn't help me to the door.

He took me to the store,

He helped me to the door.

We said our goodbyes.

With no phone on hand, all I could do was try,

Not to worry as he headed home with a sigh.

Author

Butch Raul

1-18-2014.

EMPTINESS

Nothing but a big house or a little
apartment. A writing tool and a sheet
of paper.
A place to sit with a table big enough
to hold all the tools you need.
A cup of coffee with a window to
look out, with emptiness all around.
Mind wondering thinking what it is like.
I can be bored stiff and be full of gloom,
in this empty room. Or I can give life to
my mind, and see what I can find
A book to read, there's no need. With pen
in hand I make a my stand. Put thoughts on
paper and head for the door.
Who needs doom and gloom of an empty room.

Author

Butch Raul

6-17-2006

Exercise and Dumbbells

Exercise and dumbbells
Who's exercising or
who is a dumbbell?
One can exercise
using a dumbbell wight
or one can be a dumbbell
and not exercise.
Who will get the best
Out of the word dumbbell?
Author
Butch Raul
10-23-1999

Friend Material

How to know friend material.
When that person is a friend of a friend.
One listens to them and sees what one's
friend sees.

How to know friend material.
when that person is open and honest.
One sees the truth in ones new friend.
My friend, that is you.
Author
Mildred L.Raul
9-1-2013

Friends to the End

Friends to the end.
Why must we gravel
when stormy seas we travel.
Where is that friend when
we need a warming trend.
Reaching out to hold the hand,
knowing not how to stand.
Be my friend, don't make it
the end.
Author
Butch Raul
4-29-1996

From A Boy to A Man

From a boy to a man
no one could take his
hand.
From a man to a father,
no one would even bother.

A friend to all,
who knew he would fall.
Now he's gone,
nothing to hang on to
just the empty space.
No one could take his
place.
For Zooner
Author
Mildred L.Raul
5-13-1999

From the Heart We Did Part

As words were given, the wedge was driven.
My sister stolen, life kept rolling.
A twist in your young life, caused you such strife.
A mother to me, you tried to be.
As sisters go, we did so.
From the heart, we did part.

We had a cause, clean out the garage.
Our hands did start, to tear it apart.
The phone set the pace, that day of grace.
It changed our hearts, we fell apart.
As sisters go, we did grow.
To heal the past, time to start at last.

With arms to hold close, her love ment the most.
As days went by, we cared to try.
With God in our lives, He healed the strife
One day was given, we started living.
With phone in hand, He broke the stand.

Author
Butch Raul
8-4-1997

GOD AND ANGELS

Angel's sing
As they flap their wings.
God gives us the sweetest things.

Angel's cry
When a human doesn't try,
when it's their time to die.
God's heart will always Sigh.

Angel's laugh with joy
when one gives up poise.
God has won another soul,
when we give up our earthly goals
Author
Butch Raul
6-12-2005

GOD BE WITH THE FAMILY

God be with the family
hold their hands so they
stand.
Help them in this time.
There is so much on their
mind.
Author
Butch Raul
10:00a.m.
2-22-2014

GOD DOES KNOW

Tho it's been years
we do not hear the
voice from above
from the ones we
love.
God does know
We love them so.
He wants us to
turn it around,
So we can be found.
Author
Butch Raul
10-5-2014

GOD HELP US THIS DAY

God help us this day,
God show us the way,
What should we do?
Why are we so blue?
What is this world
coming to?
It's all in the bible,
Don't be wrong.
W.W. God have done?
Clean up the best,
Where satan made the mess.
Author
Butch Raul
1-24-2013

God Is Never Far Away

Even tho we think God is far away
He told Jesus to say," "God is never far away."
We should take time to pray.
While we are in His waiting room, we tend to
be in the gloom.
We have to make our way, for what ever
comes that day.
Author
Butch Raul
12-17-2014

GOD MADE IT ALL

God made it all.
God made rain to clean the earth.
God made tears to clean the soul.
God made us to be whole.
By

Butch Raul
8-1-2014

Gone--Goodbye

Gone---Goodbye, it's been good to know ya.

Why must I try, there's no other way.

My God and I are walking away, but ask me

to stay. Where he leads is a surprise to

me I just count to three. Just on the roam

with no place to call home.

Now we're on our own and not in the zone.

Fishing and hunting for anyone who's a wanting.

Out in the field listen to what Nature yields.

It's a summers day we never go out of our way.

Author

Butch Raul

12-20-2014

HE HOLDS OUR HAND

Our God from up above
Sent down His one true love.

Jesus is the one to know,
because He'll fill our heart
and soul.

He holds our hands and guides
the way as He leads us through
the day.

It doesn't matter if it's a
light and cheery noon or a dark
and dreamy moon.

With His Angel's singing out loud,
God is watching us through the clouds.

As the world goes the wrong way,
He molds and shapes a place to pray.

With the Holy Sprit on high,
Jesus takes us to the sky.
Author
Butch Raul
1-7-1999

HE WILL LEAD US

He will lead us
Night or day,
as he teaches us
how to pray.
He will put words
to the songs as we
lean on Him all
night long.
Author
Butch Raul
12-20-2014

HEARTBREAK

The words inside
no one can hide
the time we tried
with our love out-
side to whom they
May abide.
There are no words
to take the place
of a heartbreak!
Author
Butch Raul
5-6-2006

Horses and Flowers

Horses and flowers
'tis a gift of ours.

To wallow away the day
in every way of play.

Riding through the field
watching the flowers yield.

As the horse's run in the sun
the flowers are spun.

Horses and flowers are floating
on the breeze,while the sun is
shining through the trees.
Author
Butch Raul
10-25-1998

HURRIED LIFE

I'ts a hurried life I'm living
this day God has given.
To turn me around
I don't give Him a frown.

Eternal life
What a strife.

A gift of love
From the man above.
Author
Butch Raul
7-28-1995

I Was Bored

I was bored
then I talked to the Lord.
someone said I was dead,
then I went to the Bible
and read.
My God loved me first,
So how can I do worse.
Walking through the world,
My sins He has healed.
So I can find my way back.
God don't let me lose track.

Author

Butch Raul

10-11-2002

I'll Try to Be Nice

I'll try to br nice
if you try to be smart.
then maybe no one will
have a broken heart.
By
Butch Raul
8-3-2014

I'm All by Myself

I'm all by myself,
There is no one else.
All alone in my home,
Such a mess, it hurts I guess.
Not knowing how to start,
it breaks my heart.
So much paper & envelopes
it just takes hope.
To clean this house,
I should be a mouse.
Chew it all up & put it
in a cup.
Author
Butch Raul
9-30-2014

I'm Going To God's House

I'm going to God's house today.
I'm going to God's house to pray.

With His love He says,
"I'll be with you in every way.
Look around and see, I'll stay.
So don't you go astray."

I'm going to God's house today.
I'm going to God's house to pray.

God guide me through the week.
As Your love I try to seek.
For these times are so bleak.
Author
Butch Raul
4-3-1999

In Memories

In memories to the one we love,
We love to hear their stories.
Seeing them near, as we give an
ear, to know the words so dear,
As they say them sweetly here.

We love to, see their face,
As it shows us grace.
It's like the star's fell out of
the skies and right into their eyes.
We love the touch of the one we love
`so much.
Author
Butch Raul
2-15-1985

In My Book

I'm writing all my poems in
my book
wondering how they look.
God gave them to me for
others to see.
I never know what to write.
He helps me during the day
or night.
Thanks to Him is all I can
say, because He after shows
me how to pray.
Author
Butch Raul
6-20-2014

In My Room

In my room, I'm full of gloom.
No cleaning person in sight what
a fight.
Sick again where is my friend?
I'll make a call, while the
nurse's walk the hall.
Talking and sharing lets me
know someone is caring.
Author
Butch Raul
3-10-2014

THE INDIAN MAN

The Indians we do see,
the peace maker he may be.
Stands brave and strong
while life goes on.
Hard and cruel were the
white man's rule,
that stole the land
of the Indian Man.
Author
Butch Raul
6-28-1995

Just A Note

Just a note to say, Hay! hay! hay! what a day
Going from country to country, seeing all the
dismay...
It makes people cry to see their loved ones pass by.
What to hold onto but the Lord Almighty, to help
them through the tragedy.
Author
Butch Raul
2013

JUST ME

Just me, I learned to be.

Just me is not who I am.

There are three and just me.

You see I have my God,my Jesus,

and my Comforter and they have

Just me.

With you, there could have been

us.

Only it's me and the Three.

Author

Butch Raul

4-19-2006

LEFT BEHIND

Here I am feeling down
I have such a hard time
When in this world I'm
left behind.
I'll make it soon
But cry till noon.
Author
Butch Raul
2-14-2014

Little Butterfly

Little butterfly flying so free,
how beautiful you are to me.
God made you a funny little worm,
You turned out to make us squirm
Author
Butch Raul
11-8-2014

LITTLE LADY

Little lady falling down.
Little lady lost her crown.
Little lady getting up.
Little lady found her cup.
Little lady had a frown.
Little lady got a better crown.
Little lady got a helping hand.
Littly lady took a stand.
Little lady thanked God the man.
Auther
Butch Raul
2-14-2014

LITTLE RAG DOLL

Little rag doll can you see
all the flowers on the tree
Little rag doll look at me
how I run and play in the
breeze.
Little rag doll sitting there
in your chair, without a care.
Author
Butch Raul
2006

Looking Up The Road

Looking up the road ahead,
what is that rolled in red?
A broken heart toasted over
there as no one gives a care.
Then to it you take away a
lonely one to make your day.
Looking back you seem to find
everyone is being kind until
the road does unwind.
then you find you are the one
left behind with the broken
heart.
Author
Butch Raul
8-30-1996

Lord Hear My Sigh

What a bump
Did you jump?
Lord hear my sigh,
and heal my thigh.
As I lay in my bed,
what tears I shed.
Make the pain go away,
So I can rest my head.
Author
Mildred L.Raul
7-14-2013

LORD WASH MY SINS AWAY

As I come to pray
Lord wash my sins away.
On this wonderful day.
Cleanse me in every way.
And lead me so I don't stray.
Then when this day turns to night,
be with me so it won't cause me fright.
Fill my heart with your light,
so that I will see you in the night,
and know it is a wonderful sight.
Author
Butch Raul
4-23-1999

Lost Of Life

Lost of life it could be a
husband or a wife.
There's nothing safe, no one
can take their place.
God gave us the grace, so we
don't loose our pace.
He helps us to face our day.
And we see through the haze.
Author
Butch Raul
1-22-2015

ME AND MY SHADOW

Walking down the road
just me and my shadow
look what we see.
My shadow fights with
the pain.
So what if we're walking
in the rain.
Shadow leaves me in the
dark with a broken heart.
She comes back in the
light and wants to fight.
Who can lose sight, but
we box and she never wins.
Author
Butch Raul
6-18-2006

MEETINGS AND GREETINGS

Meetings and greetings
appointments and
disappointments
miles on the road
problems to unfold.
Author
Butch Raul

Memorial Day

Memorial day is hard to see
on this day for you and me.
Going through the time,
with love ones on our mind.
It may not be the day they
left, but it still hurts us
in our chest.
Author
Butch Raul
5-26-2014

MAMA'S SMILE

Mama's smile means so much,
Mama's smile has a warming touch.
Mama's smile is fading gray.
Mama's smile is gone away.
In her place God put His grace.
I closed my eyes and to my surprise,
There was Mama's smile that meant so
much.
Author
Butch Raul
10-2-1985

ABOUT THE AUTHOR

There is a story about how I got the nick name Butch.
My brother and sister wanted to play barber and manicures.
and I was the customer. When mom got home the walls vibrated!
She gave me some money and told me to go have the barber fix it.
I marched up to the barber and showed him the
money and he asked what was he to do.
I told him to butch it off. He said "WHAT".
I said BUTCH it off. I was only seven what did I know.
So that is what he did.
I got home mom took one look at me and she turned and cried.
Then she gave me a pair of my brothers pants and said "Here Butch
put these on and give me your dress", as she gave me one of his shirt.
All that summer Mom called me Butch.

Printed in the United States
By Bookmasters